Pooh's tasty smackerels

Based on the stories by A.A.Milne

With illustrations by E.H.Shepard

D1465606

What you will find in this book

Rabbit's plan to start cooking 2	Eeyore's herby scones 13
Pooh's honey delights 4	Eeyore's surprise salad. 14
Pooh's honey and nut surprises. . . . 5	Eeyore's cheesy sticks 15
Pooh's honey biscuits. 6	Eeyore's nutty banana bread 16
Pooh's honey cream dip. 7	Tigger's spicy biscuits. 17
Pooh's honey cake 8	Tigger's malty flapjacks 18
Piglet's coconut and apple nibbles . . 9	Tigger's watercress sandwiches. . . . 19
Piglet's fruit and nut biscuits 10	Tigger's crispy crunchies 20
Piglet's coconut ice 11	Everyone's favourite drink. 21
Piglet's cup cakes 12	Rabbit's last word. 22

Rabbit's Plan to Start Cooking

Rabbit thinks that everyone should be very organised. This is a very good idea when you are going to start cooking. Rabbit likes to make plans of things to do. So, we thought we would ask him to make a special plan of all the important things to do when you are going to start cooking. Rabbit took out a pencil, licked the end of it and began to write busily:

Rabbit's order for doing things:

- Put on an apron.
- Wash your hands well.
- Read the recipe first all the way through.
- Make sure you have all the right ingredients and tools.
- Weigh and measure the ingredients carefully.
- Set out everything you need.
- Put the oven on to heat up first.
- Follow the recipe step by step.

Rabbit's list for being safe in the kitchen

1. Make sure there is an adult with you when you are cooking.
2. Ask an adult to put on the oven for you.
3. The oven is very hot so always use oven gloves to put things into the oven or take them out again.
4. Ask for help when you use a sharp knife.
5. Always hold the handle of a saucepan when you are stirring the contents. Use oven gloves with hot saucepans, too.

Rabbit's list for keeping clean in the kitchen

1. Tie back long hair before you begin.
2. Wash your hands with soap and warm water.
3. Wear an apron to cover your clothes.
4. Wash up as you work.
5. Wipe up any spills on the floor immediately.

Rabbit's list for weighing and measuring

1. Kitchen scales to weigh the ingredients.
When you are using the kitchen scales always use only grams or only ounces. Do not mix both in a recipe.
2. A tablespoon for measuring honey and syrup.
3. A teaspoon for measuring salt, pepper and spices.
4. A measuring jug for liquids.

Rabbit's Handy Hints

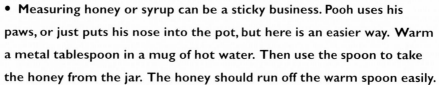

• Measuring honey or syrup can be a sticky business. Pooh uses his paws, or just puts his nose into the pot, but here is an easier way. Warm a metal tablespoon in a mug of hot water. Then use the spoon to take the honey from the jar. The honey should run off the warm spoon easily.

• If you dip a knife into a jug of warm water before use it will help smooth out the icing sugar.

• To measure margarine or butter in the packet, divide a 250g (8oz) pack of butter or margarine in half to get 125g (4oz) and then into quarters to get 50g (2oz).

• Cakes feel springy to the touch when they are cooked. Don't open the oven door too often to see if the cakes are cooked!

• Wrap sandwiches in grease proof paper to keep them fresh.

• Pooh is very tempted to dip his paws into the mixture, but try not to dip your fingers in to taste the mixture. Use a clean teaspoon and wash it before using it again.

Pooh's honey delights

Ingredients:

25g (1oz) butter, softened

1 tablespoon honey

2 ripe bananas

4 slices of brown
   or white bread

You will need:

2 small mixing bowls

wooden spoon

fork

knife

As soon as he got home, he went to the larder; and he stood on a chair, and took down a very large jar of honey from the top shelf.

1. Put the butter and honey into a mixing bowl.

2. Beat with a wooden spoon until creamy.

3. Peel the bananas and mash them in a small bowl with a fork. Add the bananas to the butter and honey and mix well.

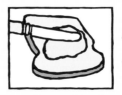

4. Spread the mixture thickly over one slice of bread.

5. Put another slice on top and cut into four pieces.

There is enough for another sandwich for Piglet.

1

Pooh's honey and nut surprises

Ingredients:

75g (3oz) butter or
margarine

6 tablespoons thick honey

4 tablespoons crunchy
peanut butter

250g (8oz) plain biscuits,
broken into crumbly pieces

You will need:

grease proof paper

small saucepan

wooden spoon

tablespoon

18cm (7in.) square baking tin

"And the only reason for being a bee that I know of is making honey."
And then he got up, and said: "And the only reason for making honey is so as I can eat it."

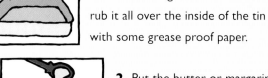

1. Grease the baking tin first of all. Put a little margarine in the tin and rub it all over the inside of the tin with some grease proof paper.

2. Put the butter or margarine into the saucepan and measure the honey into the pan.

3. Set the pan over a low heat and bring the butter and honey gently to the boil.
Stir it carefully with the wooden spoon to make sure that the butter does not burn.

• **Rabbit says take care not to splash yourself!**

4. Take the pan off the stove and mix in the peanut butter and the broken biscuits.

5. Spread the mixture into the greased baking tin and press down firmly all over with a spoon. Leave the mixture in the tin to cool. When it is cool cut it into sixteen squares.

Ideal for little smackerels when it's nearly eleven o'clock.

5

Pooh's honey biscuits

Ingredients:

250g (8oz) self-raising flour

a pinch of salt

125g (4oz) butter or
  margarine

125g (4oz) soft brown sugar

1 egg

2 or 3 drops vanilla essence

1 tablespoon honey

You will need:

1 large mixing bowl	baking tray
2 small bowls	wire cooling rack
large sieve	• **Rabbit says don't**
wooden spoon	forget the oven
tablespoon	gloves.

"It all comes," said Rabbit sternly, "of eating too much. I thought at the time," said Rabbit, "only I didn't like to say anything . . ."

Set the oven to 180°C,
350°F, Gas Mark 4

Grease the baking tray.

1. Sift the flour and the salt into one of the small bowls.

2. Measure the butter or margarine and sugar into the large mixing bowl. Beat with the wooden spoon until the mixture is soft and creamy.

3. Break the egg into the other small bowl and beat in a few drops of vanilla essence.

4. Beat the egg into the butter and sugar a little at a time and then beat in the honey.

5. Add half the sifted flour and mix until you make a soft dough. Now add the rest of the flour and make a firm dough.

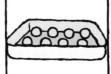

6. Roll teaspoonfuls of the dough into balls. Put eight balls at a time on to the greased baking tray. Bake for 12 minutes until golden. Then bake another eight until all the dough is used up. Cool on the wire rack.

Pooh's honey cream dip

Ingredients:

150ml (5fl oz) fresh double cream

150ml (5fl oz) yogurt

2 tablespoons runny honey

25g (1oz) chopped hazel nuts

Fresh fruit: banana, apple, grapes, orange. Eeyore might like a carrot with this.

You will need:

mixing bowl

hand beater

tablespoon

serving bowl

1. Whip the cream with a hand beater until the cream is very thick.

2. Mix the yogurt into the cream and stir in 2 tablespoons of honey.

3. Toast the hazel nuts under the grill.

• **Rabbit says use an oven glove to hold the pan. Don't have the grill too hot. Shake the grill pan to turn the nuts.**

4. Put the honey and cream mixture into the serving bowl. Spoon some honey over the mixture and sprinkle the nuts on top.

Cut the fresh fruit into pieces for dipping.

"Now let me see," he thought, as he took his last lick of the inside of the jar, "where was I going? Ah, yes, Eeyore." He got up slowly. And then, suddenly, he remembered. He had eaten Eeyore's birthday present! "Bother!"

Pooh's honey cake

You will need:

saucepan

wooden spoon

small bowl

23cm (9in.) baking tin

wire cooling rack

Ingredients:

25g (1oz) butter or margarine

6 tablespoons runny honey

175g (6oz) wholemeal flour

$1/4$ teaspoon salt

1 teaspoon mixed spice

$1/2$ teaspoon ground cinnamon

$1/2$ teaspoon nutmeg

1 large egg, beaten

$1/2$ teaspoon bicarbonate of soda

3 tablespoons milk

"I just like to know," said Pooh humbly. "So as I can say to myself: 'I've got fourteen pots of honey left.' Or fifteen, as the case may be . . ."

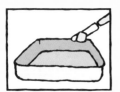

Set the oven to 180°C, 350°F, Gas Mark 4
Grease and line the bottom of the tin with grease proof paper.

1. Heat the butter and the honey together in the saucepan over a low heat and stir until the butter has melted.

2. Take the pan off the heat and add the flour, salt, spices and egg to the butter and honey a little at a time, beating until the mixture is smooth.

3. Put the bicarbonate of soda and milk into the small bowl and mix well. Stir into the mixture in the saucepan.

4. Spoon the mixture into the greased and lined baking tin. Bake in the oven for 25-30 minutes until golden. Cool for 5 minutes before turning out on to the cooling rack.

Pooh thinks he can't wait that long . . .

Piglet's coconut and apple nibbles

Grease the baking tray.

Ingredients:

175g (6oz) wholemeal flour

1 teaspoon baking powder

125g (4oz) soft margarine

1 cooking apple

50g (2oz) demerara sugar

75g (3oz) desiccated coconut

1 egg, beaten

3 tablespoons runny honey

You will need:

sieve

mixing bowl

knife and grater

tablespoon

baking tray

In the corner of the room, the table-cloth began to . . .

. . . wriggle.

Then it wrapped itself into a ball and rolled across the room.

1. Sift the flour and baking powder into the mixing bowl and rub in the margarine until the mixture looks like bread crumbs.

2. Peel, core and grate the cooking apple.

3. Stir the sugar, desiccated coconut, honey, apple and beaten egg into the flour mixture. Mix everything well together.

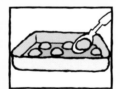

4. Put about 6 small spoonfuls of the mixture at a time on to the baking sheet, not too close together. The mixture makes about 18 nibbles.

5. Bake in the oven for about 20-25 minutes. When the nibbles are cooked place on a wire rack to cool.

Piglet's fruit and nut biscuits

Ingredients:

50g (2oz) butter or soft
    margarine

50g (2oz) caster sugar

40g (1½oz) plain flour

50g (2oz) glacé cherries

50g (2oz) almonds, flaked

You will need:

large mixing bowl

wooden spoon

knife

teaspoon

baking tray, greased

Set the oven to 190°C,
375°F, Gas Mark 5

1. Beat the butter or margarine and sugar together until soft and creamy.

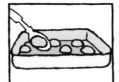

2. Sift in the flour and stir well into the butter and sugar. Chop up the glacé cherries and stir them in and then add the nuts. Make sure everything is well mixed.

3. Drop teaspoonfuls of the mixture on to the greased baking tray leaving space to allow for spreading.

4. Bake in the oven for 7-8 minutes until golden brown.

5. Allow to cool slightly, then remove from the baking tray with a flat knife and cool on a wire rack.

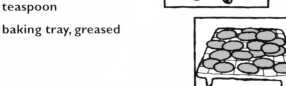

"Bother!" said Pooh, inside the jar. "Help, help!" cried Piglet, "a Heffalump, a Horrible Heffalump!"

Piglet's coconut ice

Ingredients:

175g (6oz) desiccated coconut

375g (12oz) icing sugar

5 tablespoons condensed milk

red food colouring

2 teaspoons water

You will need:

sieve

mixing bowl

wooden spoon

pastry board

plate

"Nearly eleven o'clock," said Pooh happily. **"You're just in time for a little smackerel of something."**

1. Sift the icing sugar into the mixing bowl. Add the desiccated coconut

2. Stir in the condensed milk. Use a wooden spoon to mix into a stiff paste. Add drops of red food colouring until it turns a nice pink, like Piglet's nose. If the mixture is too dry add a little of the water.

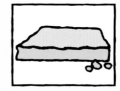

3. Put the mixture onto the board and knead until it is smooth. Shape the coconut ice into a block.

4. Dust the plate with icing sugar and leave the coconut ice on the plate for a few hours until it is firm. Then cut into small slices.

Piglet's cup cakes

Ingredients:

125 g (4oz) soft margarine

125 g (4oz) caster sugar

125 g (4oz) self-raising flour

2 eggs

You will need:

sieve

large mixing bowl

2 small bowls

wooden spoon

teaspoon

paper cases

baking tray

4. Add the flour and beaten egg a little at a time to the margarine and sugar and beat until the mixture is smooth.

5. Set out the paper cases on the baking tray. Put a spoonful of the mixture into each paper case. The mixture makes about 16 cup cakes.

6. Bake in the oven for 15 minutes until golden. When the cakes are cooked leave them to cool on a wire rack.

Set the oven to 180°C, 350°F, Gas Mark 4

1. Cream the margarine and sugar together with the wooden spoon in the large mixing bowl.

2. Sift the flour into one of the small bowls.

3. Break the eggs into the other small bowl and beat them.

Icing for the tops of the cup cakes

125 g (4oz) soft margarine

250g (8oz) icing sugar

1. Put the margarine into a large mixing bowl. Sieve in the icing sugar a little at a time, mixing well. Beat the mixture until it is soft and smooth with no lumps.

2. When the cakes are cool use a round bladed knife to spread a little of the icing over the top of each cake. You can sprinkle hundreds and thousands over the top, too.

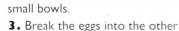

"I'm *not* Roo," said Piglet loudly.
"I'm Piglet!"

Eeyore frisked about the forest, waving his tail so happily that Winnie-the-Pooh came over all funny, and had to hurry home for a little snack of something to sustain him.

Eeyore's herby scones

Ingredients:

125g (4oz) wholemeal
   self-raising flour

125g (4oz) white self-raising flour

$\frac{1}{4}$ teaspoon salt

$\frac{1}{4}$ teaspoon ground black pepper

50g (2oz) margarine

2 tablespoons fresh herbs, chopped

125ml (4 fl oz) milk

1 tablespoon sunflower oil

You will need:

mixing bowl

measuring jug

tablespoon

pastry board

rolling pin

baking tray, greased

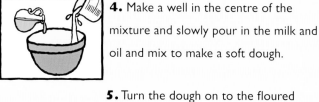

Set the oven to 160°C, 325°F, Gas Mark 3

1. Sift the flour, salt and pepper into the mixing bowl.

2. Rub in the margarine with your finger tips until the mixture looks like bread crumbs.

3. Mix in the chopped herbs.

4. Make a well in the centre of the mixture and slowly pour in the milk and oil and mix to make a soft dough.

5. Turn the dough on to the floured pastry board and shape in to a ball. Flatten the ball with the rolling pin to about 2.5cm(1in.) thick. Cut the dough into 8 sections, but don't cut all the way through the dough. Leave the dough to rest for 15 minutes in a warm place.

6. Now put the dough on to the greased baking tray and bake for 20 minutes until risen and golden. Cool on a wire rack.

13

Eeyore's surprise salad

Ingredients:

small bunch watercress

1 banana

2 small carrots

1 tablespoon olive oil

1 tablespoon lemon juice

$1/4$ teaspoon salt

$1/4$ teaspoon ground black pepper

You will need:

knife

a salad bowl

small bowl

spoon

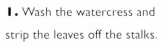

1. Wash the watercress and strip the leaves off the stalks.

2. Cut the banana into slices. Cut the carrots into thin slices.

• **Rabbit says before you use a sharp knife make sure an adult is with you.**

3. Put the watercress, banana and carrot into a salad bowl.

4. Mix the oil, lemon juice. salt and pepper in a small bowl.

5. Pour the dressing over the salad and mix together.

"Tiggers always eat thistles, so that was why we came to see you, Eeyore," said Pooh.
"Quite - quite. But your new stripy friend - naturally, he wants his breakfast . . ."

14

Eeyore's cheesy sticks

You will need:
sieve
mixing bowl
spoon
rolling pin
pastry board
baking tray

Ingredients:
125g (4oz) self-raising flour
$\frac{1}{4}$ teaspoon salt
$\frac{1}{4}$ teaspoon dried mustard
50g (2oz) margarine or
   butter
75g (3oz) cheese, grated
1 egg, beaten

"That's right," said Eeyore. **"Sing. Umty-tiddly, umty-too. Here we go gathering Nuts and May. Enjoy yourself." "I am,"** said Pooh.

Set the oven to 180°C, 350°F, Gas Mark 4.

1. Sieve the flour, salt and mustard into the mixing bowl. Rub in the margarine until mixture looks like small bread crumbs.

2. Mix in the grated cheese and add enough beaten egg to mix into a stiff dough.

3. Sprinkle flour on the rolling pin and pastry board. Roll out the dough quite thinly and cut into Poohstick size pieces. Lay out on to the greased baking tray.

4. Bake in the oven for 10-15 minutes until golden brown. Cool on a wire rack.

• **Rabbit says these can be kept in a tin if you haven't eaten them all up at once.**

Set the oven to 190°C, 375°F, Gas Mark 5

Grease and line the bottom of the baking tin with grease proof paper.

1. Mash the bananas on the plate. Beat the eggs in the small bowl.

2. Mix the sunflower oil, honey and treacle together in the mixing bowl until smooth.

3. Beat in the eggs a little at a time adding 1 tablespoon of flour with the last of the egg.

4. Stir in the rest of the flour and baking powder. Add the mashed bananas and the walnuts and mix well.

5. Spread the mixture evenly in the greased and lined baking tin.

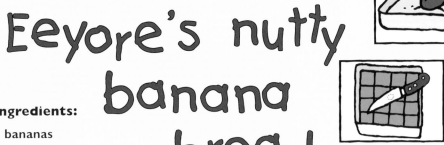

6. Bake for 20-25 minutes. Leave in the tin for 5 minutes then cut into 16 pieces. Turn out on to a wire rack to cool.

Eeyore's nutty banana bread

Ingredients:

2 bananas

2 eggs, beaten

4 tablespoons sunflower oil

1 tablespoon black treacle

2 tablespoons runny honey

125g (4oz) wholemeal flour

2 teaspoons baking powder

125g (4oz) walnuts, chopped

You will need:

plate

fork

mixing bowl

small bowl

20cm (8in.) square baking tin

"I suppose none of you are sitting on a thistle by any chance?"

"I believe I am," said Pooh.

"Ow!"

You will need:

mixing bowl
small bowl
fork
rolling pin
pastry board
biscuit cutters
baking tray

Ingredients:

250g (8oz) self-raising flour
1 teaspoon ground ginger
1 teaspoon ground cinnamon
50g (2oz) margarine
125g (4oz) soft brown sugar
2 tablespoon golden syrup
1 egg, beaten

Tigger's spicy biscuits

. . . a Friendly Tigger, a Grand Tigger, a Large and Helpful Tigger, a Tigger who bounced, if he bounced at all, in just the beautiful way a Tigger ought to bounce.

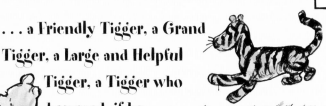

Set the oven to 180°C, 350°F, Gas Mark 4

1. Sift the flour, ginger and cinnamon into the mixing bowl. Add the sugar and the margarine. Rub all together with your fingers until the mixture looks like breadcrumbs.

2. In the small bowl beat the golden syrup and egg together with a fork. Stir into the flour mixture and mix until it makes a smooth dough.

3. Sprinkle flour onto the pastry board and the rolling pin. Press the dough flat and roll out until it is flat and quite thin. Cut out shapes with the biscuit cutters. Make a ball of any dough left and roll out flat to cut out again.

4. Space out the biscuit shapes on the greased baking tray. Bake in the oven for 8 minutes until golden brown. Then bake more of the dough until it is used up.

5. Leave the biscuits on the baking sheet until cool and hard.

Tigger's malty flapjacks

Ingredients:

50g (4oz) butter or margarine

3 tablespoons syrup

2 tablespoons malt

250g (8oz) porridge oats

You will need:

large saucepan

wooden spoon

tablespoon

20cm (8in.) baking tin

Kanga said, "Oh!" and then clutched at the spoon again just as it was disappearing, and pulled it safely back out of Tigger's mouth. But the Extract of Malt had gone.

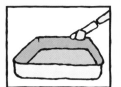

Set the oven to 190°C, 375°F, Gas Mark 5

1. Grease the baking tin.

2. Melt the butter, syrup and malt gently in a saucepan over a low heat until melted.

3. Take the pan off the heat and stir in the porridge oats.

4. Spread out in the baking tin and press down firmly with the back of the spoon.

5. Bake in the oven for about 20 minutes until golden.

6. Then cut into slices and let the flapjacks cool in the tin.

• **Rabbit says always remember to wear oven gloves to hold a hot baking tin.**

Tigger's

"Somebody BOUNCED me. I was just thinking by the side of the river when I received a loud BOUNCE."

cucumber and watercress

sandwiches

Ingredients:

4 slices bread

butter

a few slices of cucumber

some watercress

mayonnaise

You will need:

cutting board

knife

1. Spread each slice of bread with a little butter.

2. Slice the cucumber. Wash the watercress and strip the leaves off the stalks.

3. Put a layer of cucumber slices and a little watercress on one slice of bread.
Spread the other slice with mayonnaise.
Press together firmly and cut into four pieces.

Tigger likes these sandwiches with some cheese, or marmite. Roo wants a sandwich, too.

Ingredients:

175g (6oz) cooking chocolate

2 tablespoons syrup

50g (2oz) butter or margarine

125g (4oz) rice crispies

You will need:

medium size saucepan

wooden spoon

paper cake cases

Tigger's crispy crunchies

1. Break the chocolate into the saucepan, add the syrup and butter or margarine.

2. Heat very gently over a low heat and stir until melted.

• **Rabbit says the mixture will be hot. Take care not to splash yourself.**

3. Stir in the rice crispies until well covered with the mixture.

4. Spoon a little of the mixture into each paper cake case and put in the fridge to harden.

Tigger took a large mouthful of honey . . . and he looked up at the ceiling with his head on one side, and made exploring noises, and what-have-we-got-*here* noises . . .

20

Kanga said to Roo, "Drink up your milk first, dear, and talk afterwards." So Roo, who was drinking his milk, tried to say that he could do both at once . . . and had to be patted on the back and dried for quite a long time afterwards.

Everyone's favourite drink honey milk shake

Ingredients:

4 ripe bananas

3 tablespoons runny honey

4 tablespoons fresh orange juice

1 pint milk

hundreds and thousands

You will need:

mixing bowl

fork

hand whisk

4 glasses

Cooking and eating makes you thirsty . . .

1. Mash the bananas with the fork and mix in the orange juice and the honey.

2. Whisk in the milk until everything is well mixed together.

3. Pour into the glasses and sprinkle with hundreds and thousands.

Kanga adds some chopped up strawberries in the summer, as a special treat.

21

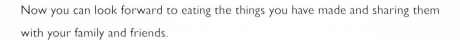

Rabbit's last word

When you have finished cooking, no matter how much you have cleared up as you go along, there is always a saucepan to wash or spoons in the sink. Did you think you would use so many cooking tools! And how did all that flour get on the floor?

Rabbit's list for clearing up

1. Wash up all the tools you have used.

2. Put everything away.

3. Clean up the table and the sink.

4. Make sure the oven and hot plates are switched off.

5. Leave the kitchen clean and tidy.

Now you can look forward to eating the things you have made and sharing them with your family and friends.

Winnie-the-Pooh and his friends, Piglet, Eeyore, Tigger, Owl, Kanga and Baby Roo and Christopher Robin will be pleased with all the little smackerels you have made. Rabbit and all his friends-and-relations will want to be invited to eat some, too.